PORCUPINES

A porcupine swimming

PORCUPINES

Wyatt Blassingame

Illustrated with photographs

DODD, MEAD & COMPANY
New York

A SKYLIGHT BOOK

Library of Congress Cataloging in Publication Data

Blassingame, Wyatt.
    Porcupines.

    (A Skylight book)
    Includes index.
    Summary: Examines the life and habits of the porcupine, concentrating on the familiar species which is found almost everywhere in North America, except in the southeastern United States.
        1. Porcupines—Juvenile literature.   [1. Porcupines]
I. Title.
QL737.R652B53   599.32'34   82-7379
ISBN 0-396-08074-X   AACR2

For Linda
My Favorite Washington Guide

Contents

A porcupine in a tree

1 The North American Porcupine

The porcupine is a strange animal.

It is small, slow-witted, and slow afoot. It doesn't see very well. Its hearing is not especially keen. It can be killed by a single blow on the nose with a club, and both men and other animals may hunt it for food. It doesn't reproduce as rapidly as most creatures its size.

But it gets along just fine anyway.

In fact, its numbers are increasing. In some places it is moving back into areas from which the growth of cities and cultivated land once drove it.

Scientifically, the porcupine is classified as a rodent. There are more than two thousand species of rodents.

The deer-foot mouse weighs only a few ounces and is one of the smallest of the porcupine's rodent relatives.

Some, like the pocket mouse, may be no more than two or three inches long and weigh only a few ounces; some, like the beaver, may weigh up to fifty pounds. But they all have four long, pointed teeth called incisors. Two are in the upper jaw, two in the lower jaw, and they keep growing as long as the rodent lives.

The beaver is the largest of the American rodents. It continues to grow throughout its lifetime and may get to be four feet long, including its tail, and weigh as much as fifty pounds. This is a mounted specimen in the Smithsonian Institution.

1 Castor canadensis, Modern Beaver

2 Beaver-gnawed Wood, Late Pleistocene Found near Fairbanks, Alaska

3 Castoroides ohioensis, extinct Giant Beaver Pleistocene skull from Lenawee County, Michigan

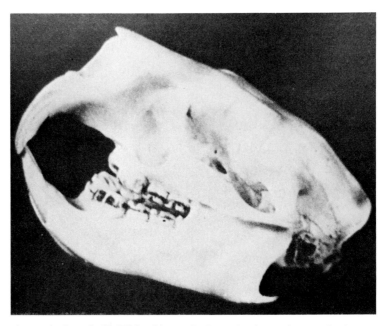

A porcupine skull. This shows the long incisors that make it possible for the porcupine to rip bark from the trunk of a tree. Then the flat, back teeth grind it up.

The porcupine's incisors make it possible for it to feed on the bark of leafless trees even in the dead of winter. But it is the porcupine's quills that make it so fascinating. Even people who have never seen a live porcupine feel sure they would recognize one, just because of those quills.

Actually, worldwide, there are many kinds of porcu-

12

pines. Later, this book will mention some of the strange Old World species. But most of this is about the North American porcupine. It may be called the Canadian porcupine, or the American porcupine, or the yellow-haired porcupine. Some people call it a quill pig, or just "porky." Scientists call it *Erethizon*. In fact, some scientists classify the yellow-haired porcupine as *Erethizon epixanthum*, and the Canadian porcupine as *Erethizon dorsatum*, a slightly different species. Under one name or the other it is found almost everywhere in North America, except the southeastern United States. Just why it doesn't live there nobody seems to know.

In the East, porcupines live chiefly in forested areas. They may make their dens in the hollow trees, or old tree stumps, much like raccoons. They are more likely, however, to make a den under a pile of rocks or beneath a tangle of fallen trees. Porcupines are not true burrowing animals, but they will make dens underground. In the Rocky Mountains they nearly always den beneath rocks. Western porcupines tend to be larger than those in the East. Some have been known to weigh thirty pounds and more.

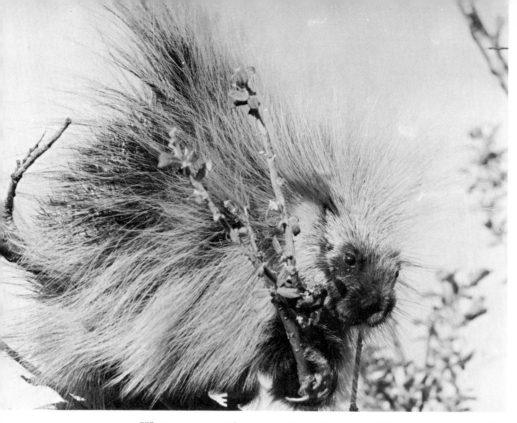

Western porcupines are often larger and lighter in color than porcupines east of the Allegheny Mountains. These are often called yellow-haired porcupines.

Most, however, will weigh less than half that much.

The Western porcupine is usually lighter in color than those in the East. These are the ones sometimes called yellow-haired. Basically they are all pretty much the same. However, some naturalists do list them as slightly different species.

2 The Quills

Most people, hearing the name porcupine, think of a mass of needle-pointed quills. Yet it is not the quills that you first see when you look at the North American porcupine. Instead, it is the guard hairs, the long, rough, darkish hairs of the porcupine's outer coat. Beneath this coat are the quills. And beneath the quills the porcupine has a coat of thick, soft, warm fur. It is this thick fur that makes it possible for a porcupine to sleep comfortably on a tree limb in below-zero weather.

But the quills are why the porcupine gets along so well despite some disadvantages.

Naturalists estimate that the porcupine has about 30,000

The back end of a porcupine. It is estimated that a porcupine has about 30,000 quills.

quills. It's doubtful if anybody every actually counted them. Donald Spencer, a research scientist for the U.S. Fish and Wildlife Service, once tried. Using a dead porcupine, he pulled 1,900 quills from just part of its tail, then quit. Later he wrote, "I was willing to accept the figure of 30,000. If an error has been made, it is probably on the conservative side."

Fed by tiny blood vessels, these needle-sharp quills will grow to be about three inches long. They cover the porcupine from its eyebrows to the tip of its tail. Only the face, legs, belly, and the underside of its tail are free of them.

Both the quills and the guard hairs are embedded in a layer of muscle and the porcupine has excellent control of them. Moving peacefully along a forest path or playing with other porcupines—and porcupines can be quite playful—the quills and hairs are held close against the body. A placid porcupine may be safely patted, as long as you don't pat against the grain.

When the porcupine is angry or in danger it is a different matter. Both the quills and guard hairs are raised upward. They stand up like the hair of a frightened girl in a comic strip.

Porcupine quills are strong enough to stick into leather, if you happen to nudge a porcupine with your shoe.

In danger, the porcupine not only raises its quills and guard hairs as a warning. It also makes a kind of grunting, growling noise, puts its nose between its feet, arches its back, and turns its rear end toward its enemy. The tail is pulled to one side, ready to strike, and this tail is the most heavily armed part of the porcupine's body.

If the danger comes still closer, the porcupine swings

18

its tail like a club, smashing it into the face or paw of the attacking animal. And that animal will usually take off, howling in agony.

The porcupine will continue its slow, untroubled way. But for its enemy, the worst is often yet to come.

When the porcupine's quills are mature they stop growing and shrink at the base. Now they are loose in their sockets. But near the tips they are covered by tiny, fishhook-like scales. Driven into the flesh of a dog or bear or some other animal, the quills pull free from the porcupine. This doesn't bother the porcupine; it will grow new ones to fill in the gaps. But for the other animal it can mean much pain and sometimes death.

Unlike the barbs of some catfish and stingrays, those of the porcupine are usually clean. They rarely cause infection. But when a wounded animal tries to brush them out of its face or paws, the tips may break off, still buried in the animal's flesh. Now the reaction of the wounded animal's muscles makes the barbed tips work deeper and deeper. Wolves, bears, even mountain lions have been found dead, killed by the quill of a porcupine that had

Panthers have been known to kill and eat porcupines. But, porcupine quills may disable or even kill the panther. Unless very hungry, the panther will usually leave the porcupine alone.

worked its way into the animal's heart or lung.

There is even one case on record of a full-grown tiger killed by the quill of an East Indian porcupine.

An animal with its mouth and tongue full of quills may be unable to eat. It may starve to death, even if the quills do not reach some vital organ.

A human being stabbed by a porcupine quill may not

20

be as badly off as a wild animal. The quills can be pulled out with tweezers—and considerable pain. But now and then a naturalist, in the excitement of capturing a wild porcupine, has been stabbed without knowing it. One scientist had the tip of a porcupine quill break off in his leg. Thirty and one-half hours later the quill had worked its way completely through the leg and was visible on the far side. A doctor removed it.

Protection against enemies is not the only benefit a porcupine gets from its quills. Very lightweight, the quills help a porcupine float like a cork on water. Using its broad feet like oars, the porcupine is an excellent swimmer.

The quills also help break the porcupine's fall when it tumbles out of a tree—but this requires some explanation.

Porky Aloft

North American porcupines spend a good part of their lives in trees, so they need to be excellent climbers. And they are. All four feet not only have strong, sharp claws, they also have rough nonskid pads that help grip the tree. And underneath the base of the porcupine's tail, there is

Porcupines are excellent climbers.

a tuft of short, stiff bristles. These serve to brace the porcupine's back end against the tree. With all four legs circling the tree, the porcupine raises its right front leg first, then its left, then pulls up both back legs together.

Instinctively a porcupine seems to know just how much weight a tree limb will hold. Feeding on the leaves and bark, it may climb out, and out—while the limb bends more and more. But almost never will the porcupine go so far that the limb will break or dump it to the ground.

In fact, almost never will an adult porcupine fall from a tree. It is the young that fall. And almost never do they fall while climbing up. Trying to get back down is the trouble.

Squirrels may race down a tree trunk just the way they went up, headfirst. Raccoons sometimes come down headfirst. But the adult porcupine comes down tail first, using the stiff bristles beneath the root of its tail as a brace.

This seems to be something the young porcupine must learn for itself. Quite often a young one starts down headfirst—and comes tumbling head over heels instead. But the quills serve to break the force of the fall, and it is rarely injured.

3 Enemies of the Porcupine

In captivity porcupines have been known to live ten years, and even more. Some may live this long in the wild. But despite its forest of needle-sharp quills, the porcupine is sometimes killed and eaten by other animals. To do this the killer must somehow turn the porcupine over to get at its unprotected belly. This is not easy because a porcupine in danger always turns to keep its heavily armored tail toward the enemy. Even so, a fox or bobcat or mountain lion will sometimes manage to get its paw under the porcupine's nose and flip it over. Or it may kill a porcupine by short, fast bites at its nose. On the other hand, the hungry fox or mountain lion is more than likely to get is mouth or paw full of quills and go limping away.

The great horned owl will sometimes kill a porcupine. It may attack so suddenly and silently out of the night that it catches the porcupine before its quills are raised. But such attacks are rare.

Porcupines feed chiefly at night, and so does the great horned owl. On its wide, softly feathered wings this owl moves in almost total silence. It may strike out of the darkness so swiftly the porcupine has no chance to raise its quills. But either by instinct or learning, most of the great horned owls seem to know the porcupine can be very dangerous. Attacks by owls do take place, but they are rare.

A fisher—the porcupine's most deadly enemy

The Fisher

It is the fisher, a close relative of the weasel and the mink, that is the porcupine's most deadly enemy.

Despite its name, the fisher doesn't like water. It rarely eats fish, unless it can steal them from some other animal. It is about three feet long, if you count one foot of tail. Its fur is brown-black in color, soft, and so beautiful it is highly prized for ladies' coats. It only weighs about ten pounds, but it is incredibly fast. It has been known to whip a dog that was trained to fight bears. And it frequently feeds on porcupines.

Exactly how the fisher attacks the porcupine is uncertain. It may not use the same method each time. Nor is it certain the fisher always wins; they have been found with quills in their paws. But at least one naturalist has watched a part of one such fight.

Robert Snyder was walking through deep woods one afternoon when he saw a porcupine asleep in an old stump. The porcupine did not move and Snyder went on with his walk. But, coming back several hours later, he wondered if the porcupine was still there. It was early twilight, about time for the night-feeding porcupine to start moving.

The porcupine was there all right, but not asleep. It was on the ground, back arched, quills raised, head down between its feet. Facing it, only a few feet away, was a fisher. Robert Snyder stood motionless, watching.

The porcupine turned its rear end toward the fisher. The barbed tail was drawn to one side, ready to strike. But it seemed to Snyder that the porcupine's movement was rather slow and uncertain.

The fisher moved as fast as a striking snake. It jumped completely over the porcupine, then whirled to face it.

Again the porcupine turned its tail toward the fisher. Again the fisher leaped over the porcupine and spun around to face it.

For several minutes this went on, the fisher leaping back and forth, the porcupine trying always to keep its tail toward its enemy. But the porcupine's movements got slower and slower. It staggered as if dizzy. Its tail dragged.

At this point Robert Snyder made an unconscious movement. The fisher saw him, whirled, and vanished in the gathering darkness.

The porcupine stayed where it was. Even when Snyder

came close, it made no move to escape. Its eyes were dull, its head not held as low and closely guarded as it should have been.

How long the contest between the fisher and the porcupine had been going on, Robert Snyder had no way of knowing. Probably for a long time, he thought. But certainly it could not have lasted much longer. The fisher would have gotten one paw under the dazed porcupine's head and flipped it over. Then one swift slash of claws would have ripped the belly open.

It is easier for man to kill a porcupine than it is for the fisher. Slow-moving, with poor eyesight, they are easy to approach. Like the skunk, they expect everything to get out of their way. Yet a single blow with a club on the porcupine's sensitive nose will usually kill it.

CAPTURING THE WILD PORCUPINE

What if you wanted to capture a porcupine alive?

For that matter, why would anybody want a live porcupine around the place? It could never be the most cuddly of pets.

Donald Spencer, who once tried to count all the quills

in a porcupine's tail, spent several years studying these animals for the U.S. Fish and Wildlife Service. He raised a number of them in his home. He found that those taken when very young did become pets. But there were problems. Being nocturnal, they were inclined to sleep in the daytime, then roam about the house all night, keeping Spencer awake. Affectionate as puppies, they insisted on climbing into his lap, or into bed with him. At such times the porcupines kept their quills carefully close to their bodies. Even so, if his hand brushed against them in the wrong direction, it could come away full of quills.

Spencer found it was easy to pick up a tame porcupine by simply putting his hand underneath the belly where there were no quills. But Spencer also learned to capture wild porcupines—and do it bare-handed!

Spencer did not use the fisher's method of always staying in front of the porcupine. Instead, he worked from the tail, the most dangerous end. But even the porcupine's tail is bare underneath. Spencer would wait for the porcupine to swing its tail. Then, before it could swing again, he would grab the tail with the palm of his hand underneath

Close-up of a porcupine's tail. With its quiver of stinging arrows, it provides a real weapon for porcupine defense.

it. His fingers and thumb, curling around the tail, could push down the barbed quills on the top.

Strangely, the porcupine almost never tried to turn and bite. Instead, it simply struggled to get away. Lifting it by the tail, Spencer could drop it in a sack and take it home to study.

Mr. Spencer did *not* recommend this as a game to be

played by anyone who happens to meet a wild porcupine. A slip, a misplaced finger, could cause serious troubles. It is even possible to get stuck by a quill without actually touching the porcupine, as we'll see. A wild porcupine is quite willing to leave people alone. And it is best left alone in return.

4 Porcupine Legends and Names

Porcupines roam the woods chiefly at night. And so, even though they are widespread and quite numerous in some places, many persons have never seen one. Or maybe they have only caught a glimpse of a porcupine in the lights of a passing automobile. But everybody has heard about porcupines. And often the things they have heard are more fancy than fact.

A porcupine cannot "shoot" its quills, as the old legend claims. If it could, Donald Spencer would never have gotten close enough to grab one by the tail. On the other hand, there is always danger in getting too close to an angry porcupine. Remember that the mature, fully grown quills are loose in their sockets. When a porcupine swings its tail

Porcupine quills are found occasionally stuck in an old log. This tells us that the animal either fell from a tree, or was noticeably disturbed by another intruder.

in anger, some of the quills may, or may not, fly out. Probably this is what gave rise to the legend of the "shooting" quills.

In his poem *The Song of Hiawatha* Henry Wadsworth Longfellow wrote that Hiawatha said:

"Give me of your quills, O Hedgehog!
All your quills, O Kagh, the Hedgehog!
I will make a necklace of them,
Make a girdle for my beauty,
And two stars to deck her bosom!"
    From a hollow tree the Hedgehog
With his sleepy eyes looked at him,
Shot his shining quills, like arrows,
Saying with a drowsy murmur,
Through the tangle of his whiskers,
"Take my quills, O Hiawatha!"

Longfellow was a better poet than a naturalist, at least
on this occasion. The porcupine cannot shoot its "shining
quills like arrows," and although porcupines are sometimes
called hedgehogs, and the two do look somewhat alike,
they are totally different, unrelated animals. The hedgehog
does have quills, but it is smaller than the porcupine, its
quills are shorter and less pointed, and it feeds chiefly on
things like insects, mice, and frogs. It lives in Europe and
there are no native hedgehogs in America.

Many people believe that when faced with danger the porcupine rolls into a ball. But here again it has been confused with the European hedgehog. In danger, the hedgehog does curl into a ball. But the porcupine, as said before, merely puts its head down low and raises its quills.

And the hedgehog can't shoot its quills either.

But Longfellow was right that the American Indians did dye porcupine quills with bright colors and use them as decorations.

The porcupine may not shoot its quills, but there is one commonly told story about it that is true. Porcupines love salt. They will eat just about anything that has salt on it. Many of the early French explorers in Canada and the Northeast traveled chiefly by canoe. Some were amazed to awake in the morning and find the handles of the canoe paddles turned to sawdust. Salt from sweaty hands had soaked into the paddles, and porcupines ate them.

Cowboys from the Northwest have had their saddles chewed into shreds. Porcupines frequently gnaw away the seats of country outhouses.

European hedgehog in protective curl

One naturalist coming face to face with a porcupine stood perfectly still. The porcupine waddled up and began to gnaw on the naturalist's sweat-stained boot.

Porcupines have been known to enter farmhouses or forest cabins and eat the tops of kitchen tables, or even eat holes in the floor where salt had been spilled.

If it's metal and the porcupine can't eat it, it will still gnaw on it, if it tastes of salt.

5 The Porcupine's Food

Remember that the porcupine, like all rodents, has four long, slightly curved teeth called incisors. These not only keep growing all the porcupine's life, but the upper and lower incisors rub against one another just enough to keep them sharp. And it is these long, sharp incisors that make it possible for the porcupine to eat happily where many other animals would starve.

Where food is plentiful the porcupine will feast on ripe fruit such as apples, plums, peaches. It may waddle slowly into a garden and stuff itself with parsley, carrot tops, green corn, strawberries. In marshy areas it will eat water lilies, arrowheads, and other water plants. In the desert it will even eat a cactus with as many quills on it as the porcupine.

Porcupine feeding

It likes flowers and will eat geraniums, petunias, asters, roses. And here is where those sharp incisors come in: the porcupine will eat the rose bush as well as the blossom.

Most porcupines, however, live in forests or heavily wooded areas without gardens or orchards. Here they feed on what is most plentiful—the trees. And it is the steady gnawing on wood that keeps the porcupine's incisors from ever getting too big, even though they keep growing.

In summer, the porcupine eats chiefly the leaves and the new, tender twigs. It tends to be a messy eater. The sharp incisors cut easily through twigs and even larger branches. Leaves and parts of the limb fall to the ground. Then deer may feed on the porcupine's leavings, particularly where the deer have already eaten all the leaves and twigs within their reach.

But porcupines, particularly when in large numbers, can do serious damage. During the winter there may be no new leaves and tender twigs available. Then the porcupine eats the bark of the tree. And it eats not only the outer bark but also the soft inner bark, called the *cambium*. In growing, a tree takes moisture and minerals through its roots.

41

These are sent up through the central core of the tree to its leaves. The leaves use them, with the aid of sunshine, to manufacture sugar and starch that goes back down the cambium layer to the roots and the trunk. If a porcupine eats the cambium all the way around a tree, the tree will die above that point.

If a tree has been scarred but not killed, the porcupine may return to it year after year. And each year it eats the bark *just above* the spot where it fed the year before. The reason is this: the sugar that comes from the leaves back down the cambium cannot pass the spot where the cambium has been eaten away. So it gathers here. Tests have shown that from twenty to three hundred times as much sugar is found above the tree's scar as below it. In fact, there will be two or three times as much sugar above a scar as there is in the cambium of an unscarred tree.

Whether the porcupine knows this by instinct or by learning is uncertain. But whenever the porcupine feeds on a tree that has been scarred in the past, it feeds just above the old scar, never below it.

A single porcupine, of course, can't do too much damage

A tree girdled by a porcupine

in a forest or even a large orchard. But sometimes they gather in much larger numbers than is commonly believed. At fruit-picking time one Maine farmer trapped sixty-five porcupines in one small apple orchard. And in a piñon forest in Colorado over 85 percent of the trees more than four inches in diameter showed the scars of porcupine feeding.

6 Migration

Even persons who know about porcupines rarely think of them as migratory. But the climate and the food supply—the same things that send birds flying south in the fall and north in the spring—also affect porcupines. Of course, the porcupine's migration is considerably different from that of most birds. An arctic tern will make a trip of about 22,000 miles, from the Arctic to the Antarctic and back again each year—a journey that would take many generations of slow-moving porcupines even if they had a way to get there.

Because of its thick, soft underfur, the porcupine can stand intense cold. When the ground is covered with snow, the porcupine has been known to climb out on a tree limb

The porcupine strips and eats the bark from tender branches of trees, as shown here.

and stay there for weeks. It sleeps most of the day and gnaws away at the bark most of the night. But if the weather and food supply—particularly the food supply— are better somewhere within the porcupine's short-legged range, it will migrate.

In many areas this migration is chiefly up or down the side of a mountain. As snow gets deep in the mountains, porcupines will move down to the valleys. A forest ranger named Walter Taylor once saw an amazing migration of literally hundreds, perhaps thousands, of porcupines. It was early winter, in the Rocky Mountains of Montana, high above the timberline. As Taylor stared in disbelief, an entire mountainside seemed to be crawling with porcupines. Probably many of them had come from miles away. Now all were moving west, away from the eastern slope of the Rockies and toward a warmer, more heavily wooded area.

Quite possibly porcupines make such a migration across this area every fall, and back again in the spring. But the place is so remote and so difficult to reach that few persons have ever seen it.

7 Family Life of Porcupines

For most of its life the porcupine is a rather solemn, silent, lonely animal. Yet now and then a whole group will get together and throw a party.

At least that's what it looks like.

It may be part of the mating ritual. On the other hand, it may happen early in the summer, well before the actual mating. A group of porcupines will come together at night. One or more may gnaw or beat at a tree stump, or even an old barrel, as if it were a drum. Other porcupines may stand on their back feet, and if they are not dancing it is easy to imagine that they are. They walk, jump, spin around. A porcupine may lie on its back, juggling a stick like a cheerleader's baton. Young males wrestle with one

A baby porcupine feeding

another, but they do it carefully, always facing one another so the quill-less bellies are together. A male may chase a female. If she doesn't want to play, she need only raise her quills and the male turns away.

Most of its life the adult porcupine is rather quiet. But in the fall, as the mating time approaches, both the males and females make thin, whining noises. This helps bring the sexes together. But it is the female that makes the choice. Once she has picked her partner, she stays close beside him. The other males leave her alone.

The actual mating usually takes place in late October or early November. The baby, called a porcupette, is born about seven months later.

And this porcupette is a most unusual creature.

PORCUPINE YOUNG

Remember that the porcupine is a rodent, and most rodents—such as rabbits and rats and squirrels—live in constant danger, preyed on by larger animals. For such species to survive, the females must bear many young every year. But the porcupine, beneath its fearful armor

A black bear may weigh 300 pounds, a porcupine about ten pounds. But a newborn bear is smaller than a newborn porcupine.

of quills, has few enemies. So the female porcupine gives birth to only one young—very, very rarely there are twins —only once a year. And that young one is able to look after itself from the start.

The adult North American porcupine will usually weigh about ten pounds. The average porcupette will weigh about one pound. An adult black bear may weigh between 250 and 300 pounds; its baby will weigh less than one pound at birth—less than the baby porcupine. In comparison to the size of the mother, the baby porcupine is one of the largest of all mammals.

The baby is born fully equipped with both quills and incisors. The quills are soft at birth, but within a half hour they are ready for action if necessary. And, amazingly, the baby knows how to use them from the first. Donald Spencer once took a baby from its mother at the moment of birth. Fifteen minutes later, never having seen another porcupine, the baby would turn its rear end toward any unusual sound or movement and lash with its barbed tail!

The baby porcupine develops rapidly in other ways. Able to walk after the first few minutes, it will follow its mother like other young animals, but only for a few days. It will nurse, but again for only a short time. Born with its long, curved incisors, it is soon able to eat grass, twigs, vegetables. Within a month it is able to feed itself completely. Within two months it wanders away, totally on its own.

A baby porcupine is able to climb trees.

Even so, there is one big difference between the adult porcupine and the young. The adults are nearly always silent, except in the mating season. The young are as noisy as most kids. They grunt, "Uh uh uh!" They squeal and whine. Much of this is obviously in play, but it may also be a kind of talk, with meaning for other porcupines.

One naturalist who had raised a number of porcupines as pets learned to make sounds just like them. One day in the woods he saw an adult porcupine asleep in a tree. The naturalist stopped and began to make porcupine noises.

In the tree the old porcupine raised its head, turned it from side to side. The naturalist stood perfectly still, and the porcupine's poor eyes noticed nothing unusual.

The naturalist kept up his noises. Slowly the old porcupine began to back down the tree. It made low, grunting, rumbling noises as it came. At the foot of the tree it stopped, still grumbling. The naturalist was no more than ten feet away, but as long as he stayed motionless, the porcupine must have thought he was just another tree.

The naturalist kept up his talk. Grumbling softly, the

old porcupine waddled forward and began to sniff at the naturalist's feet.

The naturalist moved. And the startled porcupine hurried back to its tree, scurried partway up, and waited—quills raised and tail ready.

8 Porcupines Around the World

Of all the world's porcupines, the one that looks the most "porcupinish" belongs to the scientific genus *Hystrix*. There are several species of European porcupines but, like the North American porcupine, there isn't enough difference to worry about. It may be called the African porcupine, or the crested porcupine, but whatever the name, it is quite a porcupine indeed. On the whole it is about the same size as *Erethizon epixanthum*, the North American porcupine. But the quills of *Erethizon* grow to be three or four inches long. Those of *Hystrix*, the crested porcupine, get to be fourteen inches and sometimes fifteen. When the crested porcupine raises its crest, it is something to see. The quills are not only as long and sharp as daggers, they glit-

This is a mounted specimen of the African or crested porcupine, Hystrix. *Its quills grow to a length of fifteen inches, four to five times longer than those of the North American porcupine.*

ter. They gleam in the light. The general color is dark brown, but they are silver-tipped. There are also a number of white rings below the tips. With its quills raised, the crested porcupine seems to be armed with a forest of black-and-white spears.

The crested porcupine is not only fiercer looking than its North American relative, it's also meaner. The American porcupine will defend itself, but if you leave it alone, it will leave you alone. Faced with danger, the crested porcupine will raise its fearsome quills, turn its back to the enemy, stamp its feet, and make grunting noises. This is much like the action of the American porcupine. But if the enemy doesn't retreat, the crested porcupine may suddenly charge—backwards! At this point the porcupine's enemy had best be fast on its feet, or it may be stabbed with a dozen daggers.

The crested porcupine lives in Europe, especially around the Mediterranean Sea and North Africa. Like other Old World porcupines, it lives in dens. It does not climb trees. But otherwise, its habits are much like those of the American porcupines.

THE BRUSH-TAILED AND LONG-TAILED PORCUPINES

The brush-tailed porcupine (*Atherus*) lives in East Africa and parts of Asia. It has quills all along the back and tail. Those on the tail get to be about four inches long, like those of the North American porcupine. But at the tip of the tail is a tuft of long, stiff bristles from which it gets the name brush-tailed.

The brush-tailed porcupine is about a foot and a half long, plus eight inches of tail. The long-tailed porcupine (*Trichys*) has a shorter body but a very long, fifteen-inch tail. It lives in dens that it burrows beneath rocks or bushes on several islands north of Australia.

PORCUPINES IN CENTRAL AND SOUTH AMERICA

Porcupines of the scientific genus *Coendou* may be found all the way from Mexico to Argentina. They are divided into twenty-two different species, but are all much alike. They are also much like their North American relatives, *Erethizon*, in many ways. They move about chiefly at night. They eat the leaves and bark of trees as well as fruit. They climb trees and they have needle-pointed quills from their eyebrows to their tails. But here's the difference.

The Central and South American porcupines spend even more time in trees than do the North American porcupines. They climb better, because they have one big advantage. At least it's an advantage in climbing. The last half, maybe the last two-thirds, of their tails has no quills. It is more like the tail of an opossum or a monkey. *Coendou*

A South American porcupine, with a prehensile tail

can wrap its tail around a tree limb and swing by it. The tail is not, however, a very deadly weapon. Indeed, when faced with danger, *Coendou* will stand on a tripod of its tail and hind legs, double up its front paws like fists, and growl.

LOOK-ALIKES

Porcupines are not the only animals that have developed quills for protection. As mentioned, the little European hedgehog is one. But surely the strangest of all the quill-

European hedgehog

A mounted specimen of the spiny anteater of Australia. It is not a relative of the porcupine, but it has developed quills for defense.

bearers is the echidna, also called the spiny anteater, of Australia.

Scientists call it *Tachyglossus aculeatus* and it looks even stranger than its name. Like the porcupine, it has strong claws for digging. But it also has a snout as long as its spines, and a very sticky tongue almost as long as its snout. It feeds by jabbing this sticky tongue into anthills, then bringing it back covered with ants. If the ants sting, it doesn't seem to bother the anteater.

Oddest of all, most scientists classify the anteater as a mammal. And, scientifically, all mammals are supposed to bear living young that are then nursed by the mother. The spiny anteater, however, lays eggs. But when they hatch, the female nurses them.

Although it has sharp quills, the spiny anteater doesn't rely on them for protection. Given a chance, it digs a hole and dives into it.

Altogether, there are more than forty species of porcupines around the world. But wherever you find them, porcupines have one thing in common: they are prickly characters. Without doubt, the porcupine is the pincushion champion of the animal world.

INDEX